Apertures
of
Voluptuous
Force

Poems

Sam Barbee

REDHAWK
PUBLICATIONS

Redhawk Publications
The Catawba Valley Community College Press
2550 US Hwy 70 SE
Hickory NC 28602

ISBN: 978-1-952485-63-3

Library of Congress Number: 2022933863

Cover Art entitled "Earth" by artist Leslie Karpinski.
karpinskil60@gmail.com Instagram: @leslie_karpinski_art

Also Snipes' Photography for graphics assistance.
Brian Snipes, Owner www.snipesphotography.com

Eternal gratitude to all members of numerous critique groups who, through the years, helped me find the essence of these poems, and Keith Flynn. All love to Jan.

Forward

For years I have watched Sam Barbee's progression as a poet as his lens widened, his sentences growing with vibrant imagery, each poem flashing open with a vital story only he can see. He writes like a director orchestrates a film; and I am always keen to see where he places his camera, what flushes up in his singular vision, what relationships he has discovered and sharpened by his engagement with the world. An aperture can be defined as the opening in a lens through which light passes to enter the camera. A poem's power and motion are regulated by the amount of restraint allowed to pour the right words in the right order, lending light in its engagement with the reader. Barbee's mastery as a poet is cinematic, his poems are indeed Apertures of Voluptuous Force, and as you make your way through their various musical frames you may also find they have opened new and unforgettable vistas in your imagination.

—Keith Flynn, author of *The Skin of Meaning* and editor of *The Asheville Poetry Review*

Table of Contents

I – Surface Tension

II – Peripheral Visions

III – The Long Glance

I

Surface Tension

". . . long ago, there was something in me, but now that thing is gone. Now that thing is gone, that thing is gone. That thing will come back no more."

— *F. Scott Fitzgerald, Winter Dreams*

Sunrise is Only a Question

Rain is sleep, snow pain, wind
a kiss with furtive tongue.
Read the omens before turning
to another light, its new queries,
and dawn's startle of sermons and sutras.
Darkness remains the perfected form.

Weary bartering with vile saints,
I have mellowed overnight, am wiser.
Resolved to convert era to epic, epoch to ode.
Pet my feral dread. No predator dare speak
because each understands I will leash them
to a hollow tree, promote their humiliation.

I jog the curvy road where the side-ditch
of weakness is adored – intersect a thin bridge.
Teeter out to marvel river's width, maybe
swan-dive between sink and shiver.
Or walk the far road leading to a plain
of promises where ugliness bonds

with splendor. I should confess, but to whom?
Remedies emerge from discomfort,
but hope blends a dream and a prayer.
Daybreak can transform lacking into flourish.
Decipher which questions shall be addressed,
while which others will not.

Dyslexia

Like a mad seamstress,
lightning stabs the horizon
looping trees together.
A stripe of weather
to stifle places we gather.
We shimmer down
a shining street, seething
behind the windshield of our own
dainty lives, lavender
morning glory laces the white fences.
Each tidy façade, each pane,
hides notions and tiny engines.
Near-sighted ash is blown from parquets.
An old man wears a checked shirt
sitting on his front steps, his soft hands
cradling a restless grandson in the bright plumes.

Winter Fractals

The brass knocker,
loose on our door
like a solitary fractal.
Smoke swirls in a quarry
and the day's huffing bellow

opens a portal in the storm.
My window reveals the world
I have misplaced.
Stratified sky, blue and peach.
Spring branch, cruel-pruned

by March as the white buds
tantalize and the street graces
bustle by. Rain pummels
a distant river that meanders
back and misses

the deep-seeded sprouts.
Prayer only serves as a rumor
to hammer my sweet spot
and pound all rewards.
For once, make me the gale

against their pane. Let me
reorder my words into a
blunted grace, a turbulence
of black and broken edicts,
the ruined breath of bees

and geese and every flying
thing, peering down at
the cement angels, their
cracked wings rippling
in the sunlight's frenzy.

Springtime's divine drain
yields to ash and clouds
above these broken crowns.
The last gurgles of sap
bleed sweetly out.

Raising the Mask

Each silver needle
      or lush branch
must accept shadow;
      every eye
or witless twig crooked
      by a gale.
Resculpted, as snow brings
      listening,
I scold creatures who break
      the silence,
who suppress quiet's glee.
      Weave of relics,
we are never snagged or free,
      our faces worn
smooth from raising and reaffixing
      our masks.

ADHD

No one craves madness anymore.
Peace of mind parades about . . . overrated
in the Grand Promenade. Cheaper than sleep.

A beautiful day interrupted, like
a beautiful prayer, not one of sorrow, or
petition, but for love of the status quo.

Taut at the cusp of nirvana, in a pleat of bliss,
starched and steamed, each wrinkle pressed.
Nuance tip-toes in, first venture into flight,

gnawing the fourth corner of the net,
bringing the big top down, leaving you there,
high-wired and keen to risk the first stride.

All yearn well-grounded refuge, to inhale
blooms, hear loud bees. Eager to concede
hanging within reach − but that was then,

and the urge and surge that make you leap,
pluck the fruit, kiss the girl, now kicks up a
notch, rotates backward, relaxes another axis,

and safety shrinks in the rearview. Now all
the revelries have changed. Shadows now bruises.
Rations now flavors, smiles now oozes.

Derecho

My friend calls. His wife completed chemo.
Still, he weeps, revisits loneliness.
Squall crooks cedars and pines,
coniferous faces mimicking empathy.
Tense leaves click, heave against torrents –
Morning glories refuse their reveal.

You visit friends, again . . .
and the storm wanders into
our haunted crannies as electricity flickers.
Yowl blasphemes malcontented shadows.
Neighbor's retrievers howl eager
for their routine mid-morning stroll.

In the deluge I can hear roses tremble.
Our glossy rock walk bulges puddles.
Overnight storm-front continues
to silver streets, pound trees.
Shingles blackened. Dark windows wail.
Matted squirrels track branch to branch.

I must soothe myself with telluric dreams:
we relax across grass, under sunshine, in bliss,
your allure dismisses each dumbstruck cloud.
Delightful incantation with reliable syntax –
our alchemy of alphabets fuses new shimmer
and every impure phrase is cleansed.

Frenzy

Fearrington Village
—January 2018

Among black-belted Galloway cows, and bouncing goats.
Within mews and coops. Shops. Cafés. Soothing panorama
meeting our expectations. Whitewashed fences. Staff and crook.

Then overhead,
               a discordant trumpeting.
Geese, in disjointed V's,
                    unsettle and honk,
                            circle into concentric frenzies.
Disorderly migration.
                 Heavenly havoc.
                         Perhaps misinformed
about a pond, or corn feed, or beetles,
                 they cannot regain their angle or bearing.
Their patter
             jibbers like frantic crow caw.
                  Furious screeching like mindless bats.

Here below,
communal murmur agrees for our own good,
we will search out swans.

Apple Market

Idle carts, long since unloaded,
age at the edge of the staymen orchard.
Nearby, a shelter leans, floored
with oak planks and silver leaves.
Slat baskets rock sifting autumn wind.
Silent bins are stacked behind the apple market.

A farmer props himself on boot-hewn steps
and relives crisp September evenings:
a smudge pot's flicker on his kinfolks' faces.
Skiffle tunes linger in rafter webs.
He hears their promenade's scuffing
until the last of the applejack.

He wanders out under frosted ladders
leaned against stiff boughs – apple picking is done.
The season was a dry one, harvest thousands shy
of spring's lines of credit.
Yellow jackets swarm imperfect fruit
tossed aside now sour in thatch.

Tourist traffic rumbles on the highway, rouses
the leafless hillside. Cider bottles need a dusting.
The crop, bagged and boxed, shines, customer-ready.
The tired grower summons life's courtesies,
and accepts the sunlit hours
of apple-selling before him.

Headwater

Between night showers,
my car coasts to stop.
Headlights extend over
a gray bridge into trees
diffused by tawny clouds.
White water reverberates,
shimmers below.
Between bank rocks,
I translate old tracks:
'coon and fox between
twisted glistening roots
fixed on the silver banks.
I recognize footsteps:
a clay eater dabbles
in ledge paste.
Mud-stained hands
sift silicates, vein by vein,
to extract the sweet sediment.
She splashes, washing
grit from her fingers,
and flushes her lips
with black fluid.
A doe, she strolls,
at times transfixed
by blunt headlights
across her face.

Eviction

Proud woodland scaffolds now cinders. Laurel
brittle. Stags stampede. Impending peril's
lisp brags within distraught Watauga wind.
Black bears growl inside this untaught tender,
dislodged to streams; clear waters ashed-over,
reflecting pools spoiled and sullied.

Umber veins all twist and withered roots shrivel;
blazes rage into dying of the night.
Crowning stripped, boughs flare. The whistling ribs
on fevered tongues, wrought flames' pitch bristling,
whirling, twirling, as bright ridge capstones glow.
Cedar fence rails wail for cool salve of snow.

Pasture steeds gallop, snort steam and toss
heads under hostile skyline's coarsest gloss.
My nostrils inhale fouled gust miles away;
horizons glow with firestorms through the day.
Mountain forests lie disintegrated.
Headlines for those spirits depredated.

Departure proved their alternative until
spring rainfall rejuvenates vale and hill:
dense branches and bouquets color terrain;
but no bud will flower the same again.
Timid breezes cinch, cautious to uncoil,
watching which new eternity unfolds.

Spider Faith

I see
what looms invisible
to a hexed moth:
sunlight snags
in the branch-veil.
With twig-weave
knotted under
leaf bellies,
the limber trellis
wavers,
anchored somewhere,
spires pointing
nowhere.

An ambitious night-ritual,
silver tendrils stretch,
vulnerable to
careless angels
or early-risers.
Gardeners, ventured out,
spew
and flail about
the frail sieve.
They flinch,
removing each lash
of spun salt, laced
where moth frames cure.

Hybrid

After blight, our chestnut forests
rotted. Their shadows now emerge,
suffering in furniture and mirror frames,
within unconsecrated slights of legend.

A ring of scientists now cross-breed
remaining Chestnuts with a Chinese genus,
conjuring a stubborn breed – not quite clones –
but another noble effort resistant to infection.

Wooden spooled crib where our grandchild lies
hosts our echo, a remnant thrashing
versus what life will offer, wandering on
with the deceased against what wind strikes down.

So much put asunder, crumbling stumps
rootless and toothless beneath heaven
in a forest felled in microscopic confusion,
among graves where the mighty stood.

The Versus

Where shadows lean into sun
Water trickles toward the peaks
Bats swoop into dawn
All in a land I will never see.

Upwardly-mobile incurring guilt
Reaps verses and their vengeance
Siri replaces the burning bush
Perfection permeates all I seek.

My actions contrary to those backlit
Half-baked harmonies counterpoint song
Reviling and stumbling over statutes
Italicized images for all to see.

Transmission

I crunch into evidence of last night's snowstorm, thankful
for a lone cedar accenting the corner of my motionless yard.
You stay between blankets to rethink
a New Year's Day menu.

Branch endings raw from winter amputations of color and wits,
the ice storm has finished the rest: crash-tested pines, dismantled
hardwoods – those strong of heart –
but their bitter sleep begins.

Water pipes tight, our home explores its breaking point. Snapped
power lines coil in streets. Leashed together, my dog and I
hike a favorite path up a familiar hill
no spoor of ice can conceal.

Electrical towers, stark and symmetrical, span meadow, scar forest
and brood above a crystal thicket. Mirrors sealed onto branch
endings gleam – now countable – cry and quiver in midday breeze.
Together, we have endured winter, learned how

it denies trees brief rest. At home, children trust our weave of stories
designed to dismiss questions of ashen love tethered to this season.
We must convert what bleak lessons to which victories
we choose to live without.

Much remains compromised, bruised on a frozen bough. Yearning
for dusk's whisper, when the white sheaths shrink. When spring
allows garden colors and blooms we clip to fill vases
for our houseful of tables.

Last Dance

Scream beneath bloody sunset,
as Munch on his lurch atop the colonnade.

My arms grope and grasp. Choke and gasp
as I swill remains of merlot to drown our last dance

when the wraith cut in. Distance between us
and petitions repeat: case study,

Rorschach, valentines. Solitary lunch across
from your empty black chair. With goblet salute,

a toast to pacts and pieces. Everlasting lust,
whiff of musk. Wintering, summering –

my rhythms uncontrolled as clouds wayfare –
crystalized to collaborate jeopardy.

I light the candle. Rock vacant cradle.
Much poorly timed; sweet spice, bleak hospice.

Many ways the body burns. Self-medicates.
Simmer and savor. Inhale-exhale butts into the dream.

Hunter Moon

— for that which is conceived in her is of the Holy Ghost
—Matthew 1:20

The turkey vulture straddles the centerline,
reckless, dissecting another petty death.
Wings flap wide above random meat –
rabbit, reed rat, opossum, even a cousin –
the interstate's broken yellow line hinges
rancid entrails gingered with breeze.

Fur fluffed in wind-drift, or gory pilus feathers
ruffled, fervor plateaus in a life's fading scent.
Nobility flattened, piston's impact cleansed
final breath, released a prayer, now hailed
as the least-important wheeze. Carrion
once-muscled like Job's will, holy sinew

baptized in swamp gospel. Evoked demise
delivered head-on by galvanized crown
and radials' purr speeding home. Ahead of worms,
the dead distend, abandoned to lard freeway until dust,
long after Matthew's bluster and backwater surge.
The predator, erect above history, spans

a simplified frame, strides back to grass shoulders.
Mechanized clamor reanimates the cold, white moon.
Hazed over, morning sun impersonates a twin moon:
size and shape, sizzle and gristle, duplicates dangling
like baby booties over a rearview mirror.
Both frame.

Nubbed pines rustle, limbs vanquished at the trunk,
cones cast like lots, barbed and indiscriminate.
The concrete roars with other bloody confessions
left by carcasses yanked roadside. Teeth and bone
remain − smiling, running − charming
tattered forest's specters to again incite their rage of flies.

− *October 2016*

Hurricane Force

A frenzied night courts the gale.
Its cool salve serves as the last gel
laved across my cheek,
an exhausted fog tumbling into the fields.

Hunkered in this storm's hateful gusts,
pummeled by the coercion of my flaws,
I accept this aggregate of silence
and feel a midnight fugue within.

Then it stops. . . .

Head tilted, I nudge a simple pattern
of quarried stones around my feet
once again proving I am a man without structure,
who must patiently gnaw at the wonders
abandoned by kinder wind.

Poolside, Tampa

A typhoon doused us
last night. This morning
a single crawfish
                    buoys
along the pool edge.
It scrambles from a pool boy
                            busy
netting frayed palm tree shavings.

Wedges of sunrise clabber
in the aqua shallow.
                    Chlorine boils.
Medicinal stench contorts my swallow.
I acquire a bitter rumor:
                        this rainstorm
that flushed the tropical garden
settled offshore,
                    on a starfish colony.
It upheaved thousands,
a beach-full of ocean flowers.

Fresh and nimble,
                    they wilt under
today's scorch – stubble baking,
legs curl, unsure without saltwater.
Here, in Florida,
                    midnight sky
is not the only garden
to sends its stars
crashing.

Feast

I rouse outside to whisper grievances and search
for a loving moon, but resist inclination to feast on it tonight:
my eyes squeeze tight in denial, but ease into squint.

I do hunger, perhaps will find it full and soft, easy to swallow,
not phased into a crescent rind: twin points ripe with snags
to choke me as before . . . another occasion when gnawed in regret.

Magnetic shadows lure steeled light, sop streetlamps' gilded arc.
I venture to sanctuaries of a starlit world. Appetite perks,
eager to disfigure all I once-worshiped − whether

occasions or blessings, or the deliberate defacement of heaven
I suckle the moonless skyline's swirl, pink and mottled brown,
night-gold, and imbibe shades of anything cold.

What Stone Decrees

Only weight matters in the splash.
Equates the moment.
                        Height and length
measure dimension like thunder divines
night-sky's depth,
                        like desires
intermingle cosmic dust and meteors,
share space with supernova.
                        In Antarctica,
scientists have detected astral iron
in snowdrifts. Twinkle's frigid passage
to ossified treasure –
                        compliant
to gravity's oath –
                        like copper coins
in a cold-hearted fountain. No froth
more pure than the plummet
                        and plunge
into new atmosphere –
                        like nuggets
in a brook, in riverbed's surge.
A wet reckoning
                        to round frictions –
each stone nestling into silt.

Pledge

As if numbering seasons,
the maples intuit
this could be the finale.

By September, they stand
disposed – each crook,
all succor growth

turns – lets color flash,
dismiss maudlin green
adorning cedars along the lane.

They curtsey to passers by
who discern the early change,
but pull back, saddened

when faces ignore this autumn
could conclude the promise
as the crown dies back.

Soon, a bellowing saw
will slice through recollection
of now-meaningless springs.

All color bled away
crestfallen as I walk through,
a root curled into this cold earth.

Tree Topping

Today I need tree surgeon's nerve,
and vision. Having consulted
proper manuals, second opinions
from smart neighbors,
I teeter with a rattling ladder,
tight-roping my classic lawn.

Acrophobic,
I wobble up rungs,
among crisp wafers,
shivering in September wind
and poke each limb with shears,
bump branches, watching
which twigs tremble.

One-by-one:
each severed arm drops,
biceps first, prodding wet earth,
attempting to re-root.
Surgery complete,
perched in a new fork,
nested like a sparrow,
their shredded pulp spreads
sticky on my palm.

Quiet Dust

Heaps of one-time foliage
blanket the forest floor.
The sun pierces a natural canopy:
a refuge for dying life, no human hand
to stir settlement of quiet dust.

In the self-sustaining paradise,
a patient display within each entity:
seedling to fragrance,
       acorn to tree, nipples
            replaced by streams.

A stumbling, knob-headed fawn
awakens on trembling spindles.
A supple web – aerial mosaic –
waves unheeded warning: cools steel.
Innocent temples shatter!

A smoldering pain from venery lust.
Wind blows, blood flows – vitality to dust.

The refuge, disturbed for a moment.
Order temporarily undone.
Winds will subside
and subdue remorse, again creating
a bed for the quiet dust.

Next Galaxy Over

"Things will be different
No one will lose their sight . . ."
—In the Next Galaxy - Ruth Stone

Recipients will be grateful.
Pinpricks of light bleed no treachery.
Survive the war to end all wars.
All cleansed by flawless waves of truth.

There is always awareness, then not.
Flame to ash. Sweet breeze cannot extinguish
the haughty Nero, Trump, or next shiny
autocrat – their shamble, then the quest.

We will advance without knives to twist.
No glamour, like TV's bubbling blue light,
flawless green, somber red – easily swapped
for a new horoscope. Realigned zodiac

so stars never perish alone, but chant
poet Ruth Stone's, *things will be different.*
All suffering resolved enough to cherish
like melting borders of pristine slalom snow.

My palm reads *gray sky requires loyalty*
to the dream. A doused world drowsing
after a lap dance from a woman you love:
her Holy Water the elixir of fulfilment.

I will learn to resist the etcetera. Her smile
gives in to wrinkled beauty, but with perfect teeth.
Close eyes to biases of the Old gods and the New.
Dismiss what never was, and avoid the obvious

tragedies. Hand in hand, my willing lover
and I twirl into a refreshing lake, flush ambient dust
from our ankles. I grab her and we peer beyond
questions, until things differ again.

dishonorable mention

i emerge from a pristine forest
invigorated by its vitality
but when the tallest pine topples
whose heart will console its pain,
bear that unheard demise. . . .

late-day clouds prove picturesque
abiding soft and solemn
yet when night crushes their blush
who bears the dark's stubborn weight,
the expiration of color's brawn. . . .

much to mend, much to see, yet
much to ignore of single-minded pursuits
their anguish adapted day by day
defeats fade invalidated, forfeits welcomed
and each wound converts to sufferable loss. . . .

in deafness, in blindness, when the will weakens
my nature missteps through the final race
sputters throughout this uncontested sprint
never fretting about my victory's prize
releasing the day's rivalries satisfies all.

Catch of the Day

Benched on a cedar stump
a rumpled angler listens
to the secluded brook coax:
hours of spinning whisper
from huckleberries and banks
of white flowers
warming the path back.
Wisteria gnarls curl
behind bunched lavender.
                Colorful
lures and crank bait glisten
on his khaki vest. Fatigue and fly pole
clutter the Sportsman's shadow
where his enthusiasm
dims.
      From wicker creel,
he removes a single trout.
It refuses to wrangle across his knee:
less than trophy-size, gill-dry,
fixed onyx eyes. The captor's
fingers weave it on his thigh.
He senses the vigorless fish petrify,
and tosses it into the garden's thatch.
Each pastel scale fades
in shards of afternoon.
Dusk breezes evade him,
submerged in the arbor shade.

Truth

The hill-man reared
to speak of things
he knew as sure things:
   "If a rock chimney ever leans
    away from the house,
    it always leans to the east,
    toward the sunrise."
With that revelation,
he pressed back into
his rigid slat rocker, content
   he had passed along true
   wisdom – agreed – wisdom
   of slight significance to most:
   sunrise hinges on such
truth.

II

Peripheral Visions

"Always winter, but never Christmas."

— C.S. Lewis, *Chronicles of Narnia*

Net Worth

Tracks and tannins begin the argument:
something did happen here.
Wails to stay relevant.
Birds climb from urban gloom,
pump against mortality and pinions.

Sycophants emerge from castles
trimmed with eerie parapets. Pigeons skitter.
Sidewalks of faces chase sweetbread and wine
with good sons and daughters mingling
unlike a photo: colorized,

sepia, or flushed with light.
Accounts should stay pure,
nothing taken to heart. Nothing infused.
Only newspapers and wrappers.
Busses heave and chant stilted epistles

along the ridge, toward brimming neighborhoods
where another wallowed day will be notched.
by souls who stumble on vows. Accounts
never preoccupied with clarity, abstaining
from conclusions. Chandeliers are its depravity.

The waning weep, illuminated by lampposts,
naked at bay windows. Tonight's bright moon
smaller than remembered, like a divine sea.
Strife as punctuation. Pleas and prayers.
New money steaming just ahead.

Pluperfect

Count stones in the dormant hearth,
consider liquors not to drink, caress
a matchbook of unignited arguments
news wadded under heartwood tinder.

When shall I light candles for the dead:
for broken brothers from Philadelphia,
those unwound sisters in New Orleans,
small heroes from the small town

where crosses outnumber glutted silos,
where scarecrows outnumber
children sleeping well at night,
without singing the forlorn lullaby.

Too much singing ignites my hymn
for those who were finding out
what mattered and what did not
in matters of elements and fables.

So many thoughts circle
during the moment when those chosen
gather as fettered memory
like wax from a final candle.

Three Billion Birds

—Grace Court Park
Summer Solstice, 2019

Boxwoods encircle the white gazebo and the distant
trees whisper across the tarnished copper roof.
Devoted ladies, bearing hot tea and binoculars,
search the boughs for any flash, warble or chirp.

Finding only the sun's ambition withering the park's hemlock;
dulling the bronze plaques and statues, they sit listening as
the pruned oak brush waits to become sawdust. Their teapots
and the empty branch hollows smooth each jagged wind

when nothing else eases its bite. I visit Grace Court routinely:
a dependable refuge from my pendulum of pain and watch
Old Glory ricochet against the breeze's pulse. A pedestal
clock and wrought iron rails rim the worn walkway above

the Victorian scroll and the rose beds' wilt and broken thorn.
Lesser kingdoms ply the regret in my poems and I slouch
forward, convinced we are not the last beast to matter.
Elegant brittle grass is broken between our careless toes.

Appearances

Palette, pentimento, chiaroscuro
discipline and dignity with stained fingers
swatches across white smocks, long shirts.

Noble and soothing, grace notes
adagio, intermezzo, fortissimo
gut-wrench beauty on breath, against reed.

Estrange alter-ego. Luminous idioms:
iamb, trochee, stumbling spondee
rising or falling, brazen and inviolate.

Legibility, fused volatility, scuttle
of reticent ghosts, surfacing in the moment
on the monument – the innocents.

Reformation, each sun a star
each pivot a flair, a star flare
every moon a plea: moon convenes.

The Vetting

Wind shakes droplets off autumn leaves
      sunrise dries the weakening that remain;
Walkers tethered to well-bred dogs stroll sidewalks
      pups drink water from puddles;

Siamese cats curled inside bay windows
      watch cardinals gavotte above grubs;
Sun's shimmer imparts from a distant ridge
      long leaf pines refract the crystalline rays;

Dead azaleas along the avenue shiver
      dried intent piles along concrete walls;
Sunday morning's steam off asphalt is pure
      communions partaken on rigid oak pews;

Two homeless men perch on the corner
      clothes damp beneath boughs;
Hollow men's spangled eyes look down the street
      heretics wrapped in wrong-season's vestments;

Churches adjourn and freshened well-wishers emerge
      bumper glimmer dished to those on the curb;
Rumpled, the damaged prowl where worms never die
      while the saved open menus and squint and whine.

Good Men and Glory

Thrust into bedrock,
the H-piles wring a robotic pulse,
punch sandstone stratum, stroke by
stroke, droning with fracking
what remains of the knoll,
chiming with the strain in the knell.

An immature forest in stasis,
stumped by destruction,
stunned red earth banks scraped open,
roots, stripped out into slopes, wail,
warn the rabbit and the weasel,
the wren and the rat to

flee this crime scene, no
relevant witness stepping forward.
Diesel and dump trucks the only
harbingers to blame as they ruck
to and fro, impartial to any victim,
deferring to benchmarks, and their

bastard map pinned over a subterranean
atlas and crowning this calamity.
Inexorable demons shriek and
birth girders into frothy shadows,
invite the night-shapes to free reign
of some gleaming city, erect on a hill,

with mortgaged cars and crystal cairns,
reflection shrinking the velvet moss and
blinding blue granite facades,
all now defeated by the hammer's peal:
the cacophony of echoes, station by station,
our simple ecology sealed in the fist.

Factory Girl

—Gathering of Poets
Indera Mills, circa 1900

In the basement of an early-century mill,
our coffee steams and bagels delight.
We confer in this re-purposed story
where posh carpet and fake wood-flooring
dampen our mumble and the modern dance

      of metal chairs wrenched under round tables.
      Quieted by a soundproof drop ceiling,
      fluted concrete columns support the loom's echoes
      overhead – what upper floor loads determined
      their circumference, buckling stress, thickness of base?

I sense memoirs of husbands and children and cogs
interacting with forged-steel pistons. Kinfolk weaving
linen and wools to warm anonymous realms.
Southern pine timbers cradled her immature frame
twelve hours each day, spun dust clogging both eyes,

      constricting her vision of technology's flesh.
      She lost a finger at ten, but was given the rest
      of the day off to stop bleeding. Hair matted
      with cotton fibers, she tied it back with a strip
      from a squared-off skein tossed in the refuse.

She died one Wednesday morning, sudden whimper muffled,
but was replaced by a sister, a mere absence again absorbed.
A modern chandelier now dangles above us, briefly shudders
with an unresolved pulse, like our stitches of verse,
hemming springtime fabric sewn to gallantly wear one day.

Ceded

Husks of the dead lie about
in their hotel rooms after the money has changed hands.

A few blocks over, in that neighborhood,
side of mistakes, between cluttered runnels.

No winning tickets or turnstiles, or a high-wire
strung above gravity. Easy to ignore.

No regard for angels, or insatiable demons –
just dead, content and untangled.

The last thing we remember, their tranquil stare,
beguiling us with twin cobalt moons.

Soliloquy of Cemetery Trees

Only when a grave fails to respond is a person truly dead.
Gloomy contentions, pass on like whispering ancestors did,

the tension of fictions, the dirge and diction. Sympathetic oaks
lament winter's skim of frost. Crisp slivers of brown leaves

huddle along the cemetery's crowded lanes, winter
silhouettes stiffen as winds surge and providence whips us.

Grief and love exist to disengage misspent desire; transcend flesh,
ginkgoes' guilt and guile knowing what should not be spoken.

Militant vines surround us, and entwine the fig tree with fists and knots.
Stone benches await mourners who never stray back

along the root-split path, beaded glove on the wrought iron gate.
Cherubs planted everywhere, oblige our plots, inscriptions mold

across marble. Vespers echo; a Church band's minced benediction.
Clang of spades. Frail willows eavesdrop and set forth pardons.

Dust can only speak of dust, and permit each sacred face to attend the pit,
inhale the unsullied vapor, and oblige the seraph as she inherits a final prayer.

Beams of delinquent headlights snaggle dormant branches of the dogwoods.
A granite ewe guards the last infant's stone.

True Believer

I put my trust in gravity. All the way to the grave: resting below,
shoveled-over, dust atop dust. Suspension of Disbelief has advantages . . .
can legitimize theories, Edison's first movie, moon walking, miracles –

secular or spiritual. We are all in cahoots, making it up as we tour,
through galaxies of dark matter. If we cannot wrap
our mind around misgivings, we devise specks of stuff

to prove away fear and drumbeats of doubt into shadows, pound
refuted harbingers of belief into hibernation.   Faith and Physics
have banged big again. The God Particle debate idles.

Provided with bosons, quarks, gravitons, and gluons,
no reasonable creature in a soulless cosmos could cuddle
at the speed of light and charm away belief with logic.

To extract any deity from debate makes room for this Eureka moment,
summons us down an earthen wormhole with Alice, to mew at the moon
in the great vacuum of an ever-expanding universe.

A Collider mingled devotion and quantum mechanics with
the world's awe as Coleridge challenged our cognitive estrangement,
found symmetry in a semblance of truth, conjectured the vertical

and horizontal as both breathe in shared air,
like conjoined twins' chests heaving in the night, in and out,
one heartbeat, reliant side by side.

Heads on the Wall

—America, July 5-8, 2016

All the fidgety pigeons have scattered
from ornamental squares, parking decks,
un-civil side streets, back roads. Startled
by lawless pulp of awareness, toothless patriots
recall roaming this route before, where
mud gave way to asphalt, soggy pine bridges
became concrete arches. Faces remain
unchanged: Little Miss Urban-World,
King of the Mardi Gras, Cousin of Corn,
Boy in Blue, Para-Martial Armored Ninja –

American –

ragged masses, street congregations, all
spout missives in their own stale languages,
bearing their finest bruised dreams and
blue moons, with knock-kneed approaches
to the Nation's constant set of rotten choices.
Never-ending whiff of actions rumor,
assuredly ennoble us, protect and serve us.
Each waves a sketched map, a way forward
into gray gleam where grief echoes between
two minute soap pitches and vacation condo-promos.

We have all given consent –

know every excuse by name, have bathed
in murky waters. There, in gorged distance,
bloated advantages each with gloating penance

explaining patience and understanding, claiming
rote prayers will deliver us. Routine HD horrors
ooze from widescreens, chaos interpreted
by trained-qualified-experienced professionals,
each available to media with eager frowns to again
provide instruction how to moisten the backs
of our dimmed stars and affix them overhead.

The Apogee of Voluptuous Force

Our society of faux-apologists –
Evangelists, Quacks and Duck Hunters, Politicians,
a roll call of the would-be and the has-been –
their pleas of circumstance, are noise and nostalgia.
Devising grab-bags of ill-formed excuses,
each crafts a weepy Reformation of why-and-why-knots,
seeks liberation from sin-tax. Boosted
and braced, proud in the vanguard
of rhetorical shock, living to provoke
our touchy mishmash of culture, twisting
the victim's rant, barely broken,
seeking pardon before the parachute opens.

Like a cascade of Picassos –
voluptuous force framed by brushstrokes,
cube by cube, pulsing pigment
onto slanted faces gleaming with divine
perspiration – the caffeine of America:
comprised of the camouflaged
masks of Satan, diversions parched
and fetishes parsed word by word.
Each tear a trendy faux-apogee.
Every false-promise as hygiene,
avant-garde contrition, glycerin
to lubricate the feast.

It Must Be Christmas

-- 06:30   **Wane**

Raccoons and possums never risk
moving their babies under bright moons.
As I stand at the window, drifts of starlight
collect on the sash grid.

Across the lawn, American Holly leaves shimmer.
Cedar fence shadow melts over purple vetch.
Maples and sycamores huddle
beneath Orion and Ursa Minor.

I toss my case and thermos
onto the passenger seat, and notice red eyes
peering from under the camellias, ready to scurry.
Dash lights outshine windshield stars.

A rabbit lies crushed on the broken line,
legs pointing toward the nearby stream
that flows to a culvert, then away. Corner-
by-corner, I race the sunrise downtown.

-- 07:00   **Conventional Weapons**

Colorful Buicks speckle neighborhood
Cobra heads burnish my numb street,
Another rainy morning bleeds away minutes
and distance on the crest of suburbia.

60

I pass the orphanage, mute upon a hill.
A stream separates abandoned furrows
of real estate where children endure
along the ridge, above the frostbitten meadow.

Oak and pecan sentries cower under fog.
Branches over frosted dorms provide no sanctuary.
Their stiff arms, ice-burdened, snap off.
Who nurtures static children, and hears their prayers?

They dream in a crevice, in a weave of bramble.
Yet this dawn, each must control indifference,
rely on practicing grace, armed with smiles during class,
daydreams of a warm fire, Xmas stockings stuffed
with apples and tangerines. Pecans from the grounds.

Their landscapes fade as the un-leashed glass towers approach.
Welders, belted to I-beams, burn away at girder skeletons
where pigeons collected on granite ledges, splash out
into the gray air as I admire purity of their arc and ash.

Pedestrians huddle, watching the signal change
as crosswalks reflect stoplights. I cruise
past the pruned Bradford pears cleared of nests,
swerve corners flooded with indifferent landmarks
siphoned into storm drains, choking on lively shadows.

Yellow trucks salt asphalt to beat the dead freeze.
High-rised at the bus stop, beside the Statue
to the Confederate Dead, commuters, I have come
to love, wind their watches in the dull rain.

I crane in my starched white collar
to scour every doorway, between bridge girders,
anywhere a stiff tatter of newspaper
or polyethylene might hunker.
No rusted barrels of fire. No paramedics
rattle gray hedges as the forecast grows colder.

I allow bitterness in through a sliver
of my car window, listen for faint distress.
Search for a cramped body limping through
his sleet-stung street-smart marketing.

Where is that guy in finger-less gloves,
back-lit by traffic signals? Will he
burst from a glitch? Escher sketch
emerging in a glimpse.

Nothing fills the etching I remember.
Nothing hobbles with affected wince.
Lights change. A branch splinters.
Snow polishes the parkway.

Workdays proceed. On a concrete median,
a red cord binds a bundle of papers.
Newsprint absorbs what assaults.
Front page events blur, and accounts
melt over the curb to disappear
into the street's brittle web of cracks.

Peripheral Visions

My office has comfortable furniture,
two plants, solitude a push-button away.
I imagine spring: window rolled open
to carve a slice of fresh breeze, inhale
gardenia blossoms or dogwood's blush.
A crabapple's new growth bounces
with birds all summer, courting song
above cricket's chirp in grass.

My silent pane funnels squirrel talk.
Some spruce pines' branches
sever themselves. The unfortunate
only splintered – hang twisted and frayed,
suffering life's unplanned indignity.

From time to time, a bird will sail
into my extended window. Each thud
startles me, yet the bruised fly on.
Today, a sparrow chasing the sky's reflection,
collides into tempered glass.
I witness the bird thrash in weed stalks,
frantic in discarded foliage about azalea roots,
then fade into a triangle of shadows
never to brighten.

In a pine bough: her abandoned nest waits.
As I amble to my car, a bird flutters
in sun-flare, and the outsourced shadows
veer over. I always presume the sky
is mine, even if I am adrift,
trapped naked in a distant cleft.

Coal Train

From the horizon's slit, a train yanked
by three blue-steel locomotives churns, grace intact,
toward the edge of the city. I idle . . . count coal cars –
Norfolk & Western, and Southern – each a hurdle:
a house, a garage, a microwave. My cored heart.

With one shriek, each brake works toward
one clumsy, bumping halt. In a single, unleaded fury,
car horns ignite. Wheels gridlock. Slow motion reigns.
Big trucks bully. Urban trees sway. Mothers scrutinize
watches. Millennials on phones confirm lunch dates.

 Red warnings flash. Unpolished tracks warp into patchwork
of warehouses and fast-food outlets mashed in beside them.
Johnson grass and thistles celebrate between ancient spur-lines.
Iron lanes thread to empty slaughterhouse pens, the hospital,
tobacco factories' tumbled docks, silenced mills.
The engineer, blue-striped cap pulled low, waves
at the mirage of distant blue mountains. Locomotives pump,
diesel fouling sky, rattling the bus stop.
coal cars crunch the gravel bed. Spike after spike,
crossties pucker. Flat bands of steel bend toward eternity.

It all happens at once.

Rearview-sky begins to matter. Nonlinear vista
the way we left it. Sucker punch gels my frontal lobe.
Primary as light to dark. Sand tumbles.
Shiny silicates cling. Tides ebb. Solemn deliverance,

once-upon-a-time realized as noteworthy, abandons.
Slapstick solutions falter. Gleaming façade to black.
Exhale to slouch in rude angles. Convenience
becomes climate change. Pulse, like the failure

of gravity, allows free-flying doubt. Half-life
balanced on scraps of circumstance. Switch-back
to half-truth, to false-joy: caress, then corrupt.
Palms grasp my bloodied lifeline. I try to mash slices

back into a whole. Never reclaimed, even after-life
when prayers cannot regain their edge against debate.
Holy plots with those who remain behind. Midnight
disrobes to reveal the by-products of sweat.

Erosion of the initial edifice and a lull to new rhythm.
Brutal and broken elegies. Evasion serves up its own
horror. I am left to ponder my shortchanged legacy.
Then . . . a winter bird warbles.

A Christmas tree's tin star soothes. Wet sidewalks
splash wisdoms. A good world swells. Each flower
dances under yellow sun, spirals atop the snarl,
but their hues will wither and petals will sail.

My ring's agate clanks the cup, and ale warms
to midwinter's murmur. Time to go.
Thinnest soil will prove enough to seize me.
The way we must leave it.

As if it never happened.

-- 17:30   **City Plaza**

I park on the boulevard, the day now short.
Stark spires and belfries loiter as I walk.
Stripped trees stand against wafered clouds.
At dusk, our mayor claims Christmas official:

four watts at a time, bright fruit
strung about archways and pear trees.
One tall Frazier fir bears a municipal star.
Already, there's a rumor the bulb might fail.

A brown-haired girl stands on a corner,
surrounded by pigeons. Cardinals nearby.
She digs into a sack of bread,
pitching crumbs about the concrete.

A children's choir serenades holiday favorites
as giddy taxpayers file away dismissed.
Granite gravity walls wedged along the avenue
are adorned with streetlights.

Another dusk, another heralded Yuletide,
when municipal functions proceed. A humbled
year's worth of routines compressed into scant lumens,
pastel confection sprinkled on our soft cheeks.

My day converges at a traffic signal,
where I take nothing on faith,
only cluster with others seeking
permission to proceed. I notice
a flash of rainbow slashing
the pink clouds' slow burn.

I scan for other fragments of green
and magenta refracted about the distance,
hoping to piece together the entire arch,
The horizon cluttered with empty oaks,
motionless steeples blurs.
                     More colorful
smudges might swipe away residue
of this embittered day, Redeem me
from the ravaging grind gorged
with why and why-not.

No other colorful pieces appear,
yet this single specter will prove
enough to lead me home.
Slip me out of lurking jams ahead.
It links me to my little treasures
running about the lawn,

hiding behind tawny shrubbery
like leprechauns, shimmering eyes
peeking over as I turn into the drive.
They fill in my incomplete rainbow,
scampering to me, radiant faces
exploding in unexpected light.

Carapace

Misery and her minions surface mercilessly,
stripping windows of their small rags of light.
Moon-pulse strobes behind their jagged ledge.
Twilight above my shambled edge.

An uncanny contentment rearranges
the room as I ignite a dim lamp.
Amethyst ceiling tints wallpaper of floral prints
and garish dances of leafless trees.

Taut at my desk, I align damages into stanzas.
Sheath after sheath drape the nights' losses,
quiet chilled and brittle promises.
Sundown's shawl. Constellations swell.

Revived verses, left on the stark white sill,
shroud us beneath sparkling pledges.

Lumens

A night-time map of North America's glowing hubs,
city crossroads flint and flicker

between sparse ghosts of halide mist.
Fireflies spangle across ranges,

among twinkling vagrants hitching home.
We sleep in radiance, above the plains where

glimmering omens trellis my map.
In the bright cloisters I spill my demands

onto the unlit plots. I overlay
my territories with stark light

and requisite hope. Chopping down everything
to expand sightlines, to allow

the remaining forest tossing ballads
of solemn truths. Infused in owl's

screech, midnight, explicit with stars,
clad in joules, blinks as it releases

comets and Aurora Borealis. Tinkling,
the tickled world stares back.

Snow Globe

Patterns and specific gravity.
Night looms; dense sanctions shrink.

Stilled, a test of hope, redreaming old dreams.
Each snowflake, alms for crouched beggars.
Light remains free. Shade creeps without cost.
Florid footprints frozen in snow, only capsized time after time.

A shake, a shiver, an avalanche: hypnotic fracas.

Brash and heroic vitality. Flakes buoyant.
Swirls reinvent . . . a mutiny . . . an unanswerable prayer.
Disjointed shapes longing for expansive streets, hemmed
with white-slat fences; trimmed by sleds and sleighs.

Defiant as wet wind's veil shrouds cedars and rooftops.
Continuum of what others see, desolate together, grieving as one.

Correct Posture

our perfect day – fixed-bliss inside a breeze
immaculate delight, we lounge, at ease
enchanted silhouettes that never move

stick children do not dodge their yellow ball
the living live well without casting qualm
our perfect day – fixed-bliss inside a breeze

misfits with grievous quirks and smirks abide
our skeptics frown and bloat behind facades
enchanted silhouettes that never move

surprise of birds shreds the horizon's nest
glad sun pinned high distrusts blusters' effect
our perfect day – fixed-bliss inside a breeze

your blue eyes chastise while I chirp intent
mistaking our chaste sky's slouch as consent
enchanted silhouettes that never move

you waft away and I translate your glance
the gallant knave, I mute my dissonance
our perfect day – fixed-bliss inside a breeze
enchanted silhouettes that never move

Modus Vivendi

I.

Vowels rinsed. Consonants polished.
Assonance, consonance, just trappings.
Letters arranged. Single word secrets

as fable of green leaves, sleek and slender,
nothing tenuous. Potent dominion for passing
tale's intent. Once upon a time, charming,

bound for lush horizon. Without nuance.
Sublimated to arrange lasting peace, we
must blur this day's flawed flash of vital things.

II.

Not the progress of birthdays, anniversaries.
Sunday into Saturday, warmth into terror,
flame into ash, all like a proper kiss, now a slander.

Opposites distract. Sadness gluts the void.
We caress events which once swelled the heart.
Each vacuous dance, only lovely from third person.

Favorite fruit now husk, consumed while fireworks
do magic. Stillness hints sunrise to moonless night.
Daggers gleam and protract innuendos of what remains.

III.

Content coo becomes dust. Passion fights for breath.
Seed released in praise, to avoid draught, its austerity
aware wilting awaits with dry bones' hymn. Weariness

tolled. Somber force lurks nearby. Tonal and sober.
Calamity staid, into the stream. Interrogation complete.
Explanation replete, we reach the end, unleashing

our best noun and verb. Astute arrival. Demure
denial of why we allowed downfall. Grieve no more.
Said, done, spellbound with darkness, then light.

Ticking

I forgot to wear my watch –
today of all days –
the day I hoped to correct a few things,
to be enriched at the end of the rainbow,
figure out the levy of lost love.

When I glance at my tick-less wrist,
it extends, bare and tock-less with
a vacant glare, a pale swatch
where clarity should be strapped tight:
a must for triumph on any sunlit path.

With no personal chronology, I cannot
confirm the wall clocks, or hall clocks –
hearing their disputable chimes . . .
time to go, or come, eat, sleep,
a discordant future, each peal suspicious.

Hours eroding, confidence unwound,
I realize I have mismanaged my moments –
those milliseconds that equal verve
have been altered, disordered and
garbled to the point of bedlam.

Low on day-lit instants, I concede regimen
in these seconds for which I cannot account:
dusk's toll that crowns confusion,
dark shepherd attending deceitful sheep,
idle pendulum that can never ring true.

Integrity

A shadow is a shadow on the east side of my house.
But nothing is certain on the west. Sundown
phantoms overlay faces of angels dwindling here.

Reverent, I roam crisping terrain of the early-eve
snowstorm. My flashlight reveals the crust
and crag of tracks, slices up into untarnished chill.

Sinister tendrils tighten under February's full moon,
adrift to trim silhouettes. Tighten to resist
any corrosive phase. Its pledge endures.

Common sphere beckoning its own myth:
genial dismissing wax or wane.
Hardwood tendons evade midwinter gnaw.

Holly leaves curl around their red fruit. Gleam
like frozen amulets adorning tonight's nimbus
willing to hear resilient prayers.

This slushy periphery is my cathedral, heaving
as down-wind drifts wad in eaves. Resolute
to uphold this pristine realm.

I recall Ron-Champs Chapel at dawn, each hollow
window gapes, pocking the eastern facade.
Beneath this yellow night, sky clings, bruised

and mapped in crackling trees. Wild onions
erupt, false positives across motionless lawn
like whiskers on a blind monk's cheek.

December

December orphans the dove
permits growing pains flight
whispers this is why you fought –

       in a wrap of bright cerements
       weans solstice with a mutter and a kiss
       bestows sparkle to ruined promises.

December lends diamonds
spins a symphony in crackling trees
waltzes us to the whistle of sleet –

       seizes the ripple in my weary stream
       warns a feral life knows no end
       argues reasons to abridge the verdict.

December chaperones chill
points out the joy in an ashen sky
bends all light across the gaunt branch –

       she liquors my lips with her tongue
       allows secrets loosed on a smile
       re-pours the bitter vintage till it is gone.

December is a confession
knocking down the tell-tale curtain
promising weakness will set you free –

       directs congealed communions
       palming our dead leaves as wafers
       proffer extinction in a frosty spirit
       and glazes the gravestones so I can sleep.

III

The Long Glance

*Part of you died each year when the leaves fell from the trees
and their branches were bare against the wind and the cold, wintery light."*

— Ernest Hemingway, *A Moveable Feast*

Proper Hour

Toil behind us,
cool-down before us.
This period's apt name is
evening:
        a precious interval
        when we define
        what remains
of the perfect balance
between forgiveness
and forgetting.

Benchmarks

We dispose of Christmas greenery,
box ornaments. I clear the mantel
and study you mirrored over my shoulder.
My fatigue lags, also framed there.
Winter malaise shrouds our living room –
libations so recently the norm.
I shovel Yule ash out with cinders.

After leftovers, we drive
to the cemetery to retrieve
Christmas arrangements,
considering pertinent topics:
over-spending and over-eating.
                              Ginkgo branches
sway in crisp breeze. I tighten my scarf.
You bend to straighten a festive planter
beside the cobblestone walk.
Poinsettia frames and pale carnations
decorate this grid.
                    Adorned with
faint smiles and warm fashions,
we set high standards for one another:
lovely trimmings and languages.
Withered foliage to our chests,
derivations surface, console what remains.
Dissensions arise by habit, and you
dump brown flowers
in a convenient barrel.

Blessings of Darkness

Whether from cathedral or swamp font,
offered by cleric's collar or cowl, intinction
with Communion wine or mystic's brew,
thirst always conveys new enigma to sip.

Even favorite grail can be tainted by
embittered premise: devotion to mere light,
as if darkness chokes out salvation like
scalding silence in the waterless pit.

Manger or galaxy, both sparkle. Twinkling
lamberts freeing us of fabled terrors, absolving
blunders in day-lit floundering. Any radiance
creates shadow, and for every goblin

coexists a blacked-out saint. Dove
and raven thirst for a friendly branch:
midair both hunger; each beseech
their own luminous quench.

If I think I'm in love, I am.
If I think I'm too weak, I am.
        Day or night, balanced scale,
                equal with amens, *I am*.

Godhead

A snowstorm carols, comes a hundred-nights wide.
Beamless, still bright, encasing every dark note.

False-deities slur our intimacies with brittle edicts.
They pose in costumes of caring, awash in remedies.

By morning, snowfall has christened our pasture in white.
We receive this indenture.

Even quiet happens fast now . . .
silence attempts to scribble joy into this likeness.

Milestones and benchmarks covered by flurries.
We lie back, embrace, recall once-green idioms.

The meadow stream shimmers along the treeline.
Surges escape beneath gleam.

Splotched goats kneel at the pond before their water-god
and observe inborn rituals as they sup.

Deadly Sin #8

I confront the White Bull of the page
—Ernest Hemingway

My cherry blood thuds against good judgment.
Recollection of that begrudged learned lesson
bouncing toward intuition. No reason or verse
to choose either traveled road – wind low, the season right.

Garland of tolerable routines, inside a dream of what might
have been when an alternative was clear, and clean.
I have confronted it, rhetoric from id's counsel – whispering
clever truth, nimble within my knocks and knacks.

Midnight fits and fidgets gnaw down words,
and settle nothing; though I thwart the slang
and outlive vernacular, the heroic stains matter.
There are gilded options that skirt my habits.

There are second natures that I outlast
for the instant when no reaction rings wrong.
Cathartic and comfy, I push color onto a bleached canvass.
Release myself into a cauldron of voices.

The white bull's pale stare now flush with choices.

Conversation with an Architect

What a bold poem,
           she tells me.
Winsome yet strong. Be proud.
She sparkles.
         My love is structure –
architecture.
       She is proud.

I ask her eyes, *Yes,*
          and are your designs wondrous?

She winces. *As in*
        all things,
like poems even, there are
          good and
            bad designs.

True . . . but how grand to see your structures stand!

She is silent, nodding.

I cannot wait
       to publish that first
           collection. . . .

              Why
is publishing so crucial to you?

My heart tumbles
       now knowing
the arch and single shade
        in her rainbow.

Dead Language

You rock alone on the porch
in moonlight, faint in the glow
of cigarettes and Merlot.
Ignored, another evening,
numbed, another moment
I have neglected some part of you.

Even a daring cleric reasons why
his victory prose withers on pews,
how his best blessings shrivel
as colloquial slang. I cannot claim
such gospel. Subtitles and substitutes
belittle my message.

Our seclusions waive forgiveness.
White candles burn tapered silence.
I smile, and reach to reconcile,
reveal my passion for you –
glean and glance cannot resolve
how we are separate in common spaces.

Caress which has carried us this far
retracts, craving safe distance,
into solitude, into soliloquy. One-man show
expecting no ovation, no nod, only
approval from your creaking rocker
and my wildflowers I spill about you.

What's the Point of an Opus?

To disregard simple misstep seems right,
and I hope the prodigious world forgives me.

Resemble a nomad, a modest desert father,
who sidesteps tedious conflict at all cost
to remain unburdened. Being once-removed
from most-everything,
                       I disregard
the clock's second hand – a circle,
the perfect shape until weighted with stones:
it sags, becomes less than measures
I trusted.
            The grave understands a poet.

Diorama

The funeral procession for my best friend stalls
at a traffic light. Astonished how another day departs
in tri-colored parables, I relive midnight's velocity –
shivering umber, pierced by heat lightning:
ember left in splintered oak, bough struck open,
heartwood revealed.

Today's montage, dismembered by loss, taunts
as parables chime specific. Does the grave's glint stun us?
Do we cherish its deliverance into gloom's ash,
or victory's debris to outlive myth, brittle mirth,
any muscle of fleeting affection? Blunt light compacts
into shadow, without pigment, idles beyond darkness.

Before sundown, tethered to my dog, we visit the park,
among young and capable parents, who by now
have all the answers, even advice.
My beast's growl and hearty yowl transmute
into yelps broken by bitterness
of the untangled strap.

From clouds, a sky-lit sermon sparkles, spills
its grail of crushed ice. Disarmed, I watch
wind's charisma whittle greening trees,
snuff spring's chorale, shuck fresh bark's masonry.
Backlit with multi-colors, our fatigue is christened
and blessed where these tidy sanctuaries serve us well.

Beatitude

It is winter. It is cold.
Meek sky offers no color.
Hardwood skeletons assemble
along the treeline. Roots knuckle up
through blizzard's encumbrance, grasping at sunrise.

Rhododendrons sag,
iced-over leaves weighted like
bats roosting through chill's clutch.
Snow frosts the cedars' dulled-blue berries
and skulks backside shadows as along dark edges of the moon.

I scuff out among other tracks,
across rime, to seize prioritized news.
Daffodils sprout behind liriope, fractures
splitting freeze, peaceful blessings to scatter
any ice, virtuous blooms declaring along the garden's brink.

Seedlings risen to thwart winter,
green shoots wiser than human strengths.
They shame stout men born to weakness,
those who abide in darkness, kneading the plot
where mercy must take root before fragile petals can shine.

Frozen meadowland, pitched with grass,
rams jostle and rejoice with ewes on hills,
primed for spring's shear - some for slaughter –
in the season when burnt offerings abate, and thaw
reveals bruises sealed under hoarfrost. After winter. After cold.

When Rumors Prove Enough

I spent today chasing old miracles,
green-eyed hurrahs chiding dusk.
At my mirror, I bump the reflection,
like a firefly thuds between dark branches.
For so long, I betrothed myself to wounds
like a debutante smiles through minor deaths
and diamonds: glare and blare to disable scorn.
Small plates and glasses-full that almost quench.

>I will dismiss the princely gown,
>and un-know lessons from un-grown
>days when seeking a robe and shiny sword.
>Before sleep, deliberation weighs
>the chaste against the ravished,
>fresh midnight to commemorate the journey.

Ice bakes moonlight into the pond,
expands to the reed-bed's gradual slope.
By candle's spark, I exhale, un-sober
and un-mended, weary of daylight's
irregular inflections. Distorted review.
Echo where chilly dreams still
the rowdy heart, and ready
the ladder's next rung.

Reparation

Candles soothe
by the hearth.
Spring holds
her third cup
of coffee as
we watch

the icicles weep.

The juncos warble
in kindness,
and as winter's
grip disjoints,
she reaches
for his hand.

Purge

It is not activity, but practice.
—Martin Luther

With what remains numbered, digits that flower like spring,
I long to become holy, corrected before the hour no one calls,

when proof, web-trapped, withers. For this new millennium,
I sing for those who kissed me without question.

I bleed for those who injured me. Practice patience for the harvest,
and hope to share milk and honey where pleasing words resonate.

Foretaste of drowsy morning becomes enough to dismiss sadness,
outward on a prayer, across the sheltering sky.

Peacock Alley, 1969

Summer of Sgt. Pepper, season of few shadows.
Jere wrestles the wheel of his grandma's Oldsmobile,
a 50's-something archetype. So few old enough
to drive, teenage pals with a license captained

family hand-me-downs each weekend.
We cruise the main streets, a heralded route
from The Chic-Chic to The Miljo, where
a DJ sits high in a parking lot booth spinning

45's of Vietnam and Flower-Power and pot.
I live the Southern line of popping knuckles,
spittle, pounding my fist, and gnawed fingernails.
This Friday night, Jere takes a left, off

our established route: a backstreet, dimly lit,
with incessant weeds and butts along the curb.
Thickets and thistle border derelict buildings.
A spatter of amber bulbs form a flashing arrow

barking **Peacock Alley**. The front window neon
glows *COLD BEER*. Jere strolls across asphalt,
returns with a 16 oz. Pabst Blue Ribbon.
You thirsty? He grins and shows me twin triangles

punched into the tin can crown to release a swig of manhood.
I bought one of these for Wanda last Saturday night,
before we got it on in the backseat. Go-oo-od stuff!
He presents the red, white and blue can to me

and I sip, suppressing shudder from first-beer.
It tastes reckless. *You know her sister Reba, right?*
She thinks you're real cute. You can get that.
You call it from here. Chic-Chic or Miljo? I shrug

and, he bounces the Olds over the granite curb
steering us toward 17ᵗʰ and Oleander. I peer
past the vinyl headrest into the cavernous backseat.
I twist my neck to see **Peacock Alley** in the side-view.

We laugh, and slay stoplights whether green or red.
In night-breeze, believing I am drunk proves enough.
I ponder my grandfather's '49 Plymouth, waiting
another year in our garage, to one day be all mine.

Eclipse

A lone rooster, his swollen comb flops
as he scratches and struts. Ruling
only himself during the eclipse.
Does he close his eyes . . .

consoled by a silent roost,
fear the fox skull's yowl?
He flails and tucks appetites
in a retrievable place.

In the false morn, you nap again
beneath crimson sheets. I cool on top
remembering days no sheath
could separate us. This shredded place

where we sleep, its bruised linens
will never again invite yearning.
Dawn slips past the moon.
From the fencepost, the rooster sounds.

Loveland

I would offer you Paris, next year,
or the year after – City of Lights,
Notre Dame, the Louvre, a meander
on the Seine's west bank. A drive
to the wine country, burgundy scarf
rippling in a top-down Porsche.

You have no interest being there,
but here, content surrounded
by jonquil dazzle, sipping sun tea
in shade to quench desires –
journey within your constant place,
unreachable by sea or air.

It awaits you, just outside the door,
just off the porch, barely beyond
the brick patio. You demolish
any obstacle, transport yourself,
but you take me, where lovers ache
to visit, by alternate route.

My conqueror who chases away doubt,
slays fear. Inside your garden's rusted gate,
I curl on wooden stairs, gnarled
in breeze where I never felt safe.
You wrap me in your maroon blanket
and surround me in ambience of high art.

Worm Farm

Sharecroppers peck around a shiny twenty-by-twenty
concrete slab and glare at me while nest-squawk resounds.
Jays bounce jabbing at a harvest, black and blue in my backyard.

I have sown popped-corn to appease them: I suppose
kernels might scratch any tender songbox. These migrants
ignore the filled plastic feeder that, wind-wound, spins.

I regret springtime evening serenades are no more. Perhaps
rain will patter some hollow rhythm on my state-of-the-art truss roof,
or percuss in their new birdbath. Un-absolved, I peer over the hedge,
past the fence, as my old tenants now till a neighbor's lawn.

Possum

My bound terrier nags a night shadow
wambling through high grass.
The flashlight finds blaze
of one red eye, and then a second.
In moonlight, silvery and smooth,
it squats at a wild rose thicket
fresh from a feeding next door
in the widow's garden. And I,
the reluctant killer, wield the oak handle
of a cold hoe, prepared to execute
a watchdog's bludgeoning command.
But I blink:
                    the varmint evades me,
into its familiar trough of honeysuckle,
into the night's jowl.

                    Chain taut,
the hound churns, determined
to reach and ravage the possum.
Each galvanized link twists
while she snarls her death-threat.
I silence her with my hand
and set aside the verdict.
I too am pardoned, without judgment,
and applaud the possum's escape,
coveting such cunning
as the stark promise of old age
begins to growl.
When scavenging through dark nights,
I trust safe weeds
will somehow open to welcome me.

Fresh Figs

You transplanted the sprig from your father's garden.
His communing space, where modest proverbs blessed
you and your siblings, assured you would live forever,
and would realize it all at once.

Burdened with my shadows, and the tolls autumns bring,
I pull scattered grass around the trunk. Figs hang, almost
ripe in sun: now an inheritance. You, my love, stand
fortified by this succulent memoir.

Where squirrels stripped the trunk, where a deer honed its rack,
injuries revealing green veins' shine, your fig tree survived
to re-bark itself. This morning, in our backyard, we reconvene
at the tree: re-rooted, its eight foot shadow grafts across the drive.

The tree's leaves applaud in a breeze − thank you
for deliverance − rescuing them from diesel claws snagging
their roots when wrenching up your family's homeplace.
I kneel and border your tree with cordial stones.

You forgive my poor gardening, stray fables, and splice
my fumbling indiscretions. Set aside my eviction,
now knowing your victory
all at once.

Already Passed Forever

Going directly to jail bears little consequence.
Quite calming really. Hollow pockets
increase my speed, velocity random
as I move my token. Savants tutor me

along the way: how each sacrificed their ration
debating for a throne or divination.
While there, salvation wandered away,
and wistful dust scatters over that aimless flock.

The skull remains quiet because it knows
what degrades survival skills and dignity.
The clutter of bones left visible,
no shank utters any moral fable.

Wind direction, graphed in a rose,
winnows our anthem, etches our waltz
during blue-black night. Dylan wrote: *Forever
is Such a Long Time. . . .* It proves a short time, too.

Full of idioms and idylls, tedious miles ahead
to suffer with little mastery. Wonderment
annulled by scruffy ordeals, I pack well,
including your likeness, petals softly pressed.

Body Neutral

So much to ponder relating to ruin.
In sweatpants, I sit alone in the kitchen.
Shelves full of bowls like islands floating
on a dormant sea. Recipe box closed,
but healthy appetites insist on skinny seats
at the table to debate dessert.

In striped apron vestment, by habit, I
complain about myself, even without
public shaming. I stretch tall in the window,
salivate beneath a super-sized moon.
Temptations overwhelm with insinuations
and proverbs a la mode.

This is my body: a still-life.
Pliable rules provoke me: either
with lean divinity or reflexive voodoo –
restraint's plate always wiser
than piety's platter. I want these
uneasy partnerships to reconcile.

Jekyll to Hyde; Dante to Bronte – alter-egos
shedding sandals and tight togas. My body:
the podgy regent. After a feast of regret,
I cannot resist, find room to commune,
and my caramelized hunger consumes me
as I partake pastries among amens.

Striking into Light

Isolation laps below the dock.
   Its upright angles protract the soft harbor.
A gray heron soars to the reeds. Sailboats rouse,
   mast-lights nod and a dinghy bobs in the wake.
Crests cover blackened sand, slap polished hulls:
   aft and bow, starboard and port.

Waves abrade strand around pylons, flush minute barnacles,
   dance with supple seaweed churned overnight.
Ripples deposit everything broken about the channel,
   cleansed by marsh's high tide. An empty wine bottle
whistles, lone survivor from last evening's toasts to wild youth,
   recalls dismissed offenses now distilled into pleasantries –

The heron joins me, another covert scavenger resisting sleep,
   erect and devout, prone to a bountiful strike into rising tide.
Knees crook back, twin spindles motionless, fixed akimbo
   atop stained planks. Sudden snap and flutter,
but this hunter remains still: eyes affixed
   for a silver gash of light to stab.

Tannin

Her fingers spread, darkened palms
extend to amaze and perplex me.
I surmise she paints, or prints, perhaps
has indulged a blackening craft,
or been bloodied by a joyful mistake.

She confesses her morning's sin −
harvesting a neighbor's black walnuts.
The double-hulled fruit's tears, or sap,
or sweat, had tainted her clandestine effort
with scarlet black complexities.

Blemished fingers and smudged thumb,
pretty nails rimmed with discolored cuticles,
lovely hands for a loving thrum which might
invigorate any craving, enliven my ashen
yearnings to share stains because we could.

Litmus

My wife's Hydrangea blooms again this year overwhelming
the natural-area niche I created: border of salt-treated R-R ties,
double-ground pine, fertilized to thrive in minimal sun.

Her behemoth grew from another garden's clippings overpowered
by their heft. Communal effort compromising my vision,
my devotion, my sense of how a summer backyard blossoms.

Hydrangea petition soil – poll it – task and test it to decide their hue.
Basic vs. acidic?   Unpredictable blush or blue in grubby clots –
equalizing anemic-white, icky-indigo, passionless-pink.

Voltaire gave advice: tend it – my way. That way it is <u>the</u> way,
unaltered, and unobtrusive. When I want blue, I plant blue.
Yellow shall be yellow, and red, red. Damn it! Pastels . . . ah. . . .

I decree caladiums, and lambs ear, and snap dragons. Maybe
a daisy or two. Needing predictable, I plant on, pull weeds,
prune the puny. Yet when nourished by another, as all our passions,

she has her way with me, redefines my borders, redesigns my notions.
Prompts our love for gardening to enrich a plot of untested province
blending of reds and blues, blacks and whites, and tolerates my grays.

Mirror Image

— *Mabry Mill, Blue Ridge Parkway, 1996*

      Photo by the lake:
my wife holds two bags of stone-ground flour;
our young son crosses his arms, happy, smiles on command;
younger daughter arms crossed, unhappy, because lots of things –
their scuffle like fallen leaves across the water.

      Beside the mill,
two seventy-something travelers at a split-rail fence;
hands grip top-rail, risk hickory splinters. Do they notice
our family dressed for travel . . . what might they think of us:
did we all map journey here . . . highlight a clear route home?

      This opaque day
hardened clouds cover us all. The couple's image floats
center-lake, wavering while pristine, encircled by constellations
of cast-leaves dammed-in by the mill's stone foundation
and grassy banks. We align ourselves like the water wheel;

      each hewn stone burnished,
hand-laid to hem us inside this neutral plain. Reflections ripple,
benign wrinkles – separate flocks focus south, people
to weather do's and don'ts, rights and less-rights, lost, found,
and lost. The older couple pivots. I invite my daughter to smile

      . . . persuade myself to exhale, certain all saints,
departed or gathered, wish us well.

Artificial Sweetener

Returned home from our dogma,
and clatter of careers, I might proffer
a rose or two, leave the television silent
for an air of calm, or enchantment, even
charm with chocolate and a Beaujolais.
The chemistry has been explained to me:
something can only become so sweet.
Even mounds of sugar, grains tumbling

make no potion, no mixture dollops of flesh
would not resolve. New poetry
whispered face to face could surpass.
I tender my fortunes at your shrine
when lips touch . . . us amid linen,
blended beneath a simple quilt,
with our purest recipe,
spiked with spices for the feast.

The Re-Blessed Among Us

We enter. We exit. Ignoring height
and breadth, no depth or deity can disrupt
our compact, neither the pristine nor the pious.

You know me like no other, ready to absolve fault,
pardon indiscretion. Your deft petitions codify
my daydreams with a mix of wink and wince.

We conquer this made-up kingdom, any and all.
Affection streaming over my body, you concoct
a perfect formula for pleasure wrapped in tiny pursuits.

Grand garments tear near the seam, proper welds
rip at the middle, both strongest where joined,
still deconstructed by a wayward tug.

Things Break

I broke a favorite vase.
Sweeping it into a pile,
the vase reformed, crystal
still shimmering,
dulled cuts and etchings
embracing wicked edges.

Brushed into a tighter pile,
it reassembles as another vessel,
of refraction, of fidelity,
but still a vase at heart . . .
permitting a pulse of joy
shape begetting shape.

Detriments

I pause at Cape Fear's edge
        cluttered with consonants,
                watching geese float like vowels,
all redefined, new dialect
      in laps of brackish water against banks. Roots bite
           into loam, stumps as totems standing firm.

Distance is a woman I loved,
     whispering a nocturne, lush spirit shapely in trees.
            Moored rowboats encircle piers,
bows affectionately bumping in wake.
     I watch marine creatures break the murky plain
          baptized at twilight as if simmering. . . .

Our water thrashes, tides opposing,
     toward another forever, a renowned destination
            buoying atop open water
where the delta rests . . . never frets over squall,
        disregards light or dark,
            estuary content sunup, sundown,
surging into a brined benediction whispering love burns
      forever, and we willingly commune
           as it sears us a farewell.

House Money

Each birdbath will freeze
overnight, rainwater mucked
with discarded foliage,
tiny continents anchored
to pitted cement, black tannin
contaminating each small sea.
Dry-rotting piles of maple leaves
encircle the pedestals, swallow
periwinkle, those violet blooms
now curled crust slicked over
with frost that seals their fate..
Your entire garden must collapse,
a stacked deck,
withstanding the odds,
fail at another gambit.
Another season of house money
you chose to play your hand against.

a white and quiet field

new snow about
boughs and thorns
tracks hint lairs are close.

the bleak and bare
mystical, ghostly
love a haze like a winter moon.

echoes of starlight
hushed now by drizzle
disheartened ice tumbles into crags.

i crunch into this plain
only a few inches
still quaking from your last kiss.

Timestamp

here   too late for tarot, or prayer cards,
dealt between soliloquies and regret   hear

sore   my voice veneers harsh reactions
cannot eclipse your consolations   soar

brake   yoked without burdens, edges amid us,
resolution on the brink, contours carving   break

morn   this connection between us harks
as lilies trolling sun for rain   mourn

rest   my withering veins, bothersome brain, lost
memory begrudged like yearning   wrest

sewn   laughter our soundtrack, a flute's elegance
into elation of brass, timbre of camber   sown

feat   probe of eyes, a French kiss, a French hiss
in my ear, releases tonight's gavotte   feet

presence   collapse hush, share our song with clouds
constellations emerge, we collect them   presents

knot   our dread of saying *I love you* never
supplants the hollowness when we do   not

Jazzland and Jericho

I wear a newborn, baby-blue shirt
and it shouts love me like there is
no day or night. We are here with

dirge-yellow wallpaper and dim lamps
as the silence whines unfed.
You, my favorite tune, pause

like a wind-swayed fern,
poised at half mast. My music must
have a name and surpass any genre.

Put down your latest popular novel
and hold my hand. We will
dial the radio to Jericho, to jazzland,

to jubilee, and demolish the discreet.
We will traverse any gutter or trough
of sagging sleep. We can escape

where it is always twilight, and I will
adorn you with yet another diamond
scarf and darker glasses. My chariot

is right outside, ready to charge
through calamity's jeweled tinsel.
Hurdle this sunset with me.

Acknowledgements

The Poet wishes to thank the following magazines, journals, and anthologies where these poems, or versions of them, appeared.

Adelaide: Deadly Sin #8; and Net Worth

American Diversity Report: Body Neutral

Appalachian Edge: Headwater

Appalachian Journal (Appalachian State University): Lumens

As It Ought to Be: Hybrid (Pushcart Nominee)

Asheville Poetry Review: Jazzland and Jericho; Peacock Alley; Three Billion Birds; and What's the Point of an Opus

Atlantis Magazine (University of NC-Wilmington): Quiet Dust

Bayleaves (NC Poetry Council): Spider Faith

Burningword Literary Review: Detriments

California Quarterly: Loveland

Coastal Plains Review: Nimbus; and Poolside, Tampa

Crucible: Transmission

Deep South Magazine: Hunter Moon

Exquisite Pandemic: Pluperfect; Appearances; The Vetting; Bound Papers; and Apogee of Voluptuous Force

Flying South Magazine: Carapace; Godhead; Modus Vivendi; Hands to Myself; and Mirror Image

Grand Little Things: Soliloquy to Cemetery Trees

Hermitfeathers: Appearances

Kakalak: Next Galaxy Over

Klecksograph: What Stone Decrees

Literary Yard: Diary of Demise

Macrina Magazine: Last Dance

Main Street Rag: Conversation with an Architect; Pluperfect; Good
     Men and Glory; and Heads on the Wall

Medusa's Kitchen: Dead Language; and Things Break

North Carolina Literary Review: December

O.Henry Magazine: December

Old Mountain Press: Eviction; and It Must Be Christmas

Poetry South: Factory Girl (Pushcart Nominee)

Potato Eyes: Possum

Randall Jarrell (Finalist): Diorama

Red-Headed Stepchild: Litmus

Saint Andrews Review (Sam Ragan Tribute): Truth

Silver Birch: Sunrise is Only a Question

Snapdragon: Snow Globe; and When Rumors Prove Enough

Streetlight Magazine: Beatitude

The Courtland Review: Feast

The Pangolin Review: Striking into Light

The Poetry Box: True Believer

Verse-Virtual: Benchmarks

Voices on the Wind: Already Passed Forever

Vox Poetica: Ticking

Wellspring: Apple Market

*Weymouth Center "ExperieNCe Poetry" (National Poetry Month
     Celebration):* Proper Hour

Wild Goose Poetry Review: Catch of the Day

Word Doodles: Raising the Mask; and Wane

About the Author

Sam Barbee has three collections of poetry. His two most recent are *Uncommon Book of Prayer* (2021, Main Street Rag), and *That Rain We Needed* (2016, Press 53), which was a nominee for the Roanoke-Chowan Award as one of North Carolina's best poetry collections of 2016.

His poems have appeared recently in *Poetry South, Literary Yard, Asheville Poetry Review, Appalachian Journal,* and *Adelaide Literary Magazine*, among others; plus on-line journals *American Diversity Report, Exquisite Pandemic, The Voices Project*, and *Medusa's Kitchen.*

He is a two-time Pushcart nominee; was awarded an "Emerging Artist's Grant" from the Winston-Salem Arts Council to publish his first collection *Changes of Venue* (1997, Mount Olive Press); has been a featured poet on the North Carolina Public Radio Station WFDD; received the 59th Poet Laureate Award from the North Carolina Poetry Society for his poem "The Blood Watch".

He has served as President of the Winston-Salem Writers, and North Carolina Poetry Society, and is one of the originators of the Poetry In Plain Sight – now in its tenth year -- a poetry initiative to feature NC poets on broadside posters and display them in NC towns statewide.

About the Cover Artist

North Carolina native Leslie Karpinski has spent her lifetime painting, drawing, and creating as an artist. With a formal education from East Carolina University from the Painting and Drawing Department, Leslie's work is an exploration of her love for nature, seeing the beauty in all living things combined with the process of painting, drawing, mixed media, surface design and whatever else brings out her creative spirit! She is currently painting a body of work which explores hiking trails, mountains and our coastal communities

Contact Leslie at karpinskil60@gmail.com

www.ingramcontent.com/pod-product-compliance
Lightning Source LLC
Chambersburg PA
CBHW071141090426
42736CB00012B/2188